THIS CANDLEWICK BOOK BELONGS TO:

_____

_____

_____

_____

JOLLY ROGER

and the Pirates of Captain Abdul

Colin McNaughton

CANDLEWICK PRESS
CAMBRIDGE, MASSACHUSETTS

PART I: *Roger's Plight*

You didn't argue with Roger's mom. She may have been a tiny little thing, but Roger's mom was a fearsome lady. Yes, siree!

This is Roger's mom.  What a miseryguts!

What a grump. What a sourpuss!

Our story begins with Roger doing the shopping in the port that lay over the hill from his home. Roger, as usual, was feeling sorry for himself. It was work, work, work, morning till night, and he was fed up.

What was it his mom had said? Four pounds of vinegar and a bottle of carrots? No, that couldn't be right. Two yards of cheese and a quarter pound of elastic? "Oh, rats!" cursed Roger. "I've forgotten. Now she'll be mad at me again. I wish my dad was home. Life wouldn't be so bloomin' hard if he hadn't run off and left us."

Roger slouched, muttering, along the quayside.

"Good mornin', Jolly Roger!" said a passing youth. "What are you looking so crab-apple grumpy about? Lost a doubloon and found a penny, eh? Ha, ha!"

All the people in the village called Roger 'Jolly' Roger because he always looked so miserable. (No, Roger didn't think it was very funny either.)

Perhaps at this point I'd better explain about Roger's dad. Roger's dad had disappeared when Roger was just a baby. That's why Roger's mom was so sad and miserable all the time. Roger's dad had been a farmer, but one year there had been a terrible drought, so Roger's dad became a sailor. But (and here's the sad part) on his first voyage, his ship had come back without him. Completely dadless! He had last been seen talking to a pack of pirates in an inn on the Barbary Coast (a terrible place full of the sort of people your mom's always warning you about!) late one night and he had not returned to his ship when it sailed on the morning tide.

"Reckons 'e was lured away wi' tales o' Spanish gold!" said one of his shipmates glumly to Roger's mom. Reckons 'e's bin an' gone an' joined the pirates! Reckons 'e'll never be seen again! Reckons . . . "

...Yes, all right!

"Yes, all right!" interrupted Roger's mom. "We get the picture!" And she had not smiled from that day onward.

When the news spread, people cried "Poor Roger's mom!" and "Poor baby Roger. What will become of them? It'll be the workhouse for them." (Miserable crowd, aren't they?)

Right enough, life was very hard in the years that followed, for in those days there was no welfare and their bank account was, I'm afraid, quite bare. But somehow they struggled on.

Roger was turning all this over in his mind when he reached the grocery store. As he was going in, he noticed a large scruffy piece of paper stuck up in the window. In the most awful handwriting you can imagine (your teacher would have a fit!) this is what he read:

Just the job!

JOYN THE PIRATES
— cabin boy rekwired
FOOL TRAYNIN GIVIN.
HOPERTOONHITY 4 TRAVIL
GUD PROMOSHUN PROSPEX
NO SOFTEES KNEED APPLY
SEE ABDUL the SKINHEAD
CAPTIN of the GOLDEN BEHIND his mark Oooh arrgh!

"That's it! I'll run away to sea and join the pirates, and maybe I'll find my dad," thought Roger, getting excited. "And when I grow up and I'm all huge and hairy and covered in scars and my pockets are bulging with treasure, I'll come back and say 'Ha!' to my mom. 'Ha and fiddle-dee-dee! Take that! And that!' . . . "

While Roger was busy pretending to slice up his mom like a salami, he failed to notice (good thing too, he would have had kittens!) a rowing boat gliding across the harbor toward him with an evil *schloop, schloop, schloop*. It was filled with such a pack of horrible, dirty, smelly, ugly, hairy, scary men as the world had ever seen. (Well, *this* part of the world anyway!) They oozed and slithered, as they had been taught at pirate school, out of the boat and up onto the quay.

Without so much as an
"'ow do y'do?'" or an "Excuse
me"—only "'e'll do!", they stuffed
(yes, stuffed) young Roger into a sack!
Then they disappeared over the quayside
into their boat and schloop-schlooped
back to their ship, which was moored
just outside the harbor mouth.

Roger struggled all the
way, like a ferret down
a trouser leg.

PART II: *Kidnapped! Oooh-aargh!*

When he was tipped out of the sack, Roger found himself surrounded by pirates, all of whom, he noted, had parts missing—fingers, eyes, ears, even legs!

"Belay below thar, me wee barnacle! Curse thee fer a lubbock squirt! Ah-ha! Oooh-aargh!" bellowed a great big ugly brute whom Roger guessed to be the captain, as he seemed to have more parts missing than anybody else. "Hold all! Blast thee! What be that a-grundlin'-bad-bilgy stench, eh, young feller-me-lad? Eh? Be that ye a-stinkin'? Eh? Oooh-aargh!"

"I'm sorry," said Roger, "but can't you speak English? I thought this was an English pirate ship. I didn't know I'd need foreign languages."

"HINGLISH!!!" stormed the captain. "Shiver me tonsils and avast me wooden leg. Oooh-aargh! A-coursen I speaks the Hinglish, ye hinsolent fish 'ook! Why, fer a ha'porth o' tar I'd slit yer mizzen mast! Blast ye from yer keel t'yer crow's nest! Aye! Curse thee! I'll lash yer stern wi' a cat-o-nine-tails! Oooh-aargh! That I will! Ha, har! Oooh-aargh!"

(All pirates at this time in history spoke in this strange way. No one seems to know why. One theory is that it was because they were extremely stupid.)

"Charming!" said Roger, who was beginning to understand the lingo and did not altogether like what he was hearing. "Well, you didn't have to kidnap me. I was just about to come over and apply for the job anyway."

"Oh, I'm most frightfully sorry," said the captain, forgetting himself for a moment and being polite. "Jest a cursed minute," (remembering himself again) "what, by the doubloons o' the Barbary Corsairs, be that disgusting stench a-waftin' 'cross me poopdeck?"

"It be the smell o' the cursed soap, Cap'n," said one of the pirates. "It's the wee landlubber here. He stinks of it! Yes 'e do. Oooh-aargh!"

As the smell of "nice and clean" began to penetrate those awful hairy pirate nostrils, there were cries of "Pooh!" and "Pass me a clothespeg afore I'm sick!"

"So," said the captain, "yer after bein' a pirate eh, soapy chops? What be yer name? Curse thee! Ye smelly sprat! Oooh-aargh!"

"It's Roger, actually," said Roger.

"Ha, har!" laughed the pirates.

"Rogeractually! What sorta name be 'Rogeractually'? That baint no use, blast yer breeches! Ha, har! Oooh-aargh!"

"No," said Roger patiently, "not 'Rogeractually,' just Roger."

"Well, me little soapsud," said the captain, "makes no odds, it still be a useless name, that it be. Oooh-aargh! If ye wants ter be a pirate, me boy, ye needs a nickname, ha-har! That ye do. Oooh-aargh, by gunpowder!"

"And what, pray, is a nickname?" asked Roger in a tone of voice which made it quite plain that he didn't take kindly to someone saying his name was useless.

"'What be a nickname?' sez 'e. A nickname, me wee plank, be a name that tells people what sort of person ye are. That it be! Curse yer thick skull! An' ye can't be a proper pirate wi'out a nickname. Baint that the truth, me hearties, eh? Oooh-aargh! Ha, har!"

"Aye, Cap'n, that be the truth," replied the crew as one man.

"Line up, ye swabs, and we'll hintroduce our smelly selves. Ha, har! We'll tell 'im the sort o' nicknames real pirates have. Oooh-aargh! Curse ye all! Ha, har! A-one an' a-two an' a-one, two, three!"

I shall have a fishy...

And this is what they sang, in very loud, tuneless voices . . .

'Jolly' Roger.

"Well!" said Roger, giving them a round of applause. "I suppose I do have a nickname of sorts. The people around here call me 'Jolly' Roger, because they think I look so miserable all the time."

"'JOLLY' ROGER!" roared the pirates. "That be perfeck! Ha-har!" (Well, *they* thought it was funny. A pirate would, you see: A 'Jolly Roger' is another name for the skull and crossbones—the pirate flag, but you probably knew that already.)

When they'd finished ha-har-ing, Captain Abdul asked Roger why he was so miserable.

"My mom," said Roger to the pirates, who were all ears (well, maybe not *all* ears, as some had the odd one missing),

'Jolly' Roger! That be perfeck!

"my mom is the cleanest, tidiest person in the whole world! And she wants me to be just like her. Every day it's the same—up before dawn, make the bed, clean my room, get washed (here there were cries of horror from the pirates), comb my hair ("WHAT'S A COMB?"), eat my breakfast, wash the dishes, bake the bread, brush my teeth (*GASP!*), churn the butter, scrub the floors, iron the clothes, clean the pigsty, wash the cow, polish the goat, shampoo the chicken, whitewash the coal—on and on and on!" (Well it was almost true, thought Roger, crossing his fingers behind his back.)

There oughta be a law!

"Poor wee scab!" growled the captain. "Oooh-aargh! It ain't right fer a lad t'be brought up s'clean! By the curse of Portuguese Bart! Tain't natural like! No, kids should be smelly and 'orrible! 'Tis the only chance they gits afore they grows up inter people! The on'y chance that be, oooh-aargh, unless they become pirates, ha-har! Then they can be dirty, smelly, lazy, an' 'orrible all their lives! Ya-har! Curse y'all! Oooh-aargh! Ya-har!"

This fine speech by the captain was much appreciated by his crew, who cheered him and cried such things as "Yeah, that's why I joined up!" and "I'll drink t'that!" and "Down wi' soap!"

"That there mother o' yourn needs t'be taught a lesson! And we be just the chappies to be a-doin' it!" growled Abdul. "What sez 'ee, me shoal o' sharks, eh? Should we go an' shiver 'er timbers?"

The crew replied with cries of "Aye!" and "Sounds okay to me."

And so the pirates went, as pirates do, a-cursing and a-swearing, a-hooting and a-hollering, enough to give a fellow a rather nasty headache.

As they swarmed into the rowing boat, Abdul the Skinhead shouted to the only member of the crew left on board, "Cookee! You stay 'ere an' look after me ship. Watch out fer customs men an' traffic wardens, curse their satchels! An' give the lad some grub. The poor wee groat needs a-buildin' up if 'e's going to be a pirate. By the powers! That 'e do!"

The pirates pulled toward the quay, the captain waterskiing behind.

Back on board *The Golden Behind* (you can probably guess what the figurehead was! If you can't, I'm not going to tell you. It's far too rude!) Cookee took Roger down to the galley (that's a kitchen to us landlubbers) and threw together a little something in a white wine sauce with sautéed potatoes.

Roger wolfed it down.

"Come on now," said Cookee. "I'll take you down to the stores an' get you kitted out."

The stores, deep in the hold, had the sort of things you'd find on any pirate ship of the time—nothing unusual.

"Cookee," said Roger, "why didn't you have a song?"

"Oh, that's because I'm not a proper pirate, young Roger. Oh, dear me, no. I'm only the cook. Anyway, you can't have a song without a proper pirate nickname an' I don't even have a real name. Y'see when I was kidnapped I was knocked on the noodle an' I lost my memory. The cap'n made me cook an' gave me the name 'Cookee,' as I couldn't remember my own."

He paused, then added, "If y' really wants to know, I do have a private song o' my own. I'll sing it to you if y' promise not to laugh.'

"I promise," said Roger, and Cookee sang his song.

Is there anybody out there
    Who might know this little man?
Is there anybody out there
    Who can tell me who I am?

Can you tell me what my name is?
    Can you tell me where I'm from?
Was it Plymouth, York, or London?
    Am I Harry, Dick, or Tom?

Was I rich and was I famous,
    Was I poor, was I unknown?
Have I children and a wife somewhere,
    Or did I live alone?

Is there anybody out there
    Who might know this little man?
Is there someone, somewhere
    Who can tell me who on earth I am?

"Poor Cookee, that's the saddest thing I've ever heard," said Roger, wiping a tear from his eye.

"Aye, well there's nothin' t'be done about it, so come on, try these on for size," and he handed Roger a little pirate outfit.

Roger put it on and said, "That's more like it! Now I look like a real pirate!"

PART III: *Roger to the Rescue*

Cookee and Roger waited for the beastly buccaneers to return. They waited and waited. And then they waited some more. They waited three whole days and then, suddenly—nothing! No sign. Not even a postcard. ("What could have happened?" I hear you ask.) Roger thought they should go and find out. Cookee agreed. So off they went.

They hitched a lift from a passing fisherman, ran through the town, and cautiously crept up to the wall surrounding Roger's home. They saw Roger's mom with a cutlass in one hand and a pistol in the other. More weapons were slung over her shoulders and around her little waist. There was something strangely familiar about the men milling around her.

"It's the cap'n and his crew!" whispered Cookee, astonished.

"But it can't be," said Roger, "they're all so . . . clean!" And, sure as five twos are ten, there stood Abdul the Skinhead and his crew: clean, tidyish, combed and . . . working!

Hop in!

'Portobello' Billy and 'Yardarm' Pitts were milking the cow.

'I'm Alright' Jack was watering the vegetables. Abdul himself was digging up turnips (not easy with a wooden leg)!

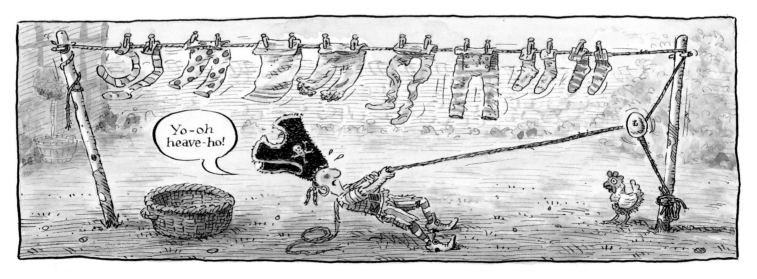

'Poop-deck' Percy Ploppe was hanging out the washing.

'Hard-hearted' Henry Hawkins was sawing firewood. 'Riff-raff Rafferty was mending a hole in the chicken run.

Walker 'the Plank' was on the roof fixing a leak.

'Bully-boy' McCoy was bullying a chicken into laying an egg. 'Spanish' Omar Lette was cleaning the windows.

Last of all, the massive figure of Khan 'the Really Nasty,' dressed in a frilly apron, was washing the dishes at the well.

"Psst! Khan!" Roger hissed. "What happened?"

"Jolly Roger!" said Khan. "We be captured! Every man jack o' us!"

"But how?" asked Roger. "There are eleven of you and only one of her!"

"Khan not sure," said Khan. "But when we got here we shut 'er in the house and started 'avin' some pirate fun. Well then, yer mom, curse 'er tonsils, calls out in a high an' girly sort o' voice, 'Oh no! I hope they don't find the barrel of rum hidden behind the barn door.' 'Yo-ho!' cries us. 'We 'eard that!' Well, we finds the rum an' has a party. We got drunk as lords an' when we woke up we found ourselves a-chained 'and an' foot. Since then it's been terrible! First she made us wash. Then she put us to work! An' every night she chains us up in the barn. It's awful! We be a-doomed! A-DOOMED!"

"KHAN!" came the voice of Roger's mom. "Haven't you finished that washing up yet? You lazy barbarian!"

"Almost done, ma'am," replied Khan in a weedy little voice.

"Ye'd better go!" he whispered to Roger. "We told 'er we'd kidnapped ye an' she says 'nless we tell 'er where y'are, she's goin' t' twist our ears off!"

Roger crept back to where Cookee was hiding and told him the bad news.

"We must help them!" said Roger. "I know what she's like: she doesn't miss a trick. They'll never escape on their own!"

Secretly, Roger was rather proud of his mom. He knew he would be in for it if she caught him helping the pirates. But he had to help them. After all, it was his fault they were here in the first place.

"Right," said Cookee, "but we' better wait until it's dark."

The light in Roger's mom's bedroom had been out for hours before Roger and Cookee dared to make their move.

"Follow me," whispered Roger. "There are some loose boards around the back of the barn. She may be watching the front."

Quiet as ships' cats they slid through the darkness and into the barn.

"Soap!" hissed Cookee. "The smell o' 'nice and clean'!"

He and Roger crept over to the herd of slumbering pirates.

"Captain!" said Roger, shaking Abdul the Skinhead.

As the captain dredged himself out of dreams of keelhauling old ladies,
he grunted, "Curse thee! Avast! Who be a-distubin' o' me beauty sleep? Fer a
ha'porth o' tar I'll slit 'is grunge lubbock! Oooh-aargh!"

"It's all right," said Cookee to a startled Roger, "he's like this every mornin'
when I takes him his Rice Krispies soaked wi' rum. He hates being woken up."

Roger found the keys hanging on a hook and set the pirates free. He
pushed open the barn door and whispered, "Let's go, but don't make a sound."

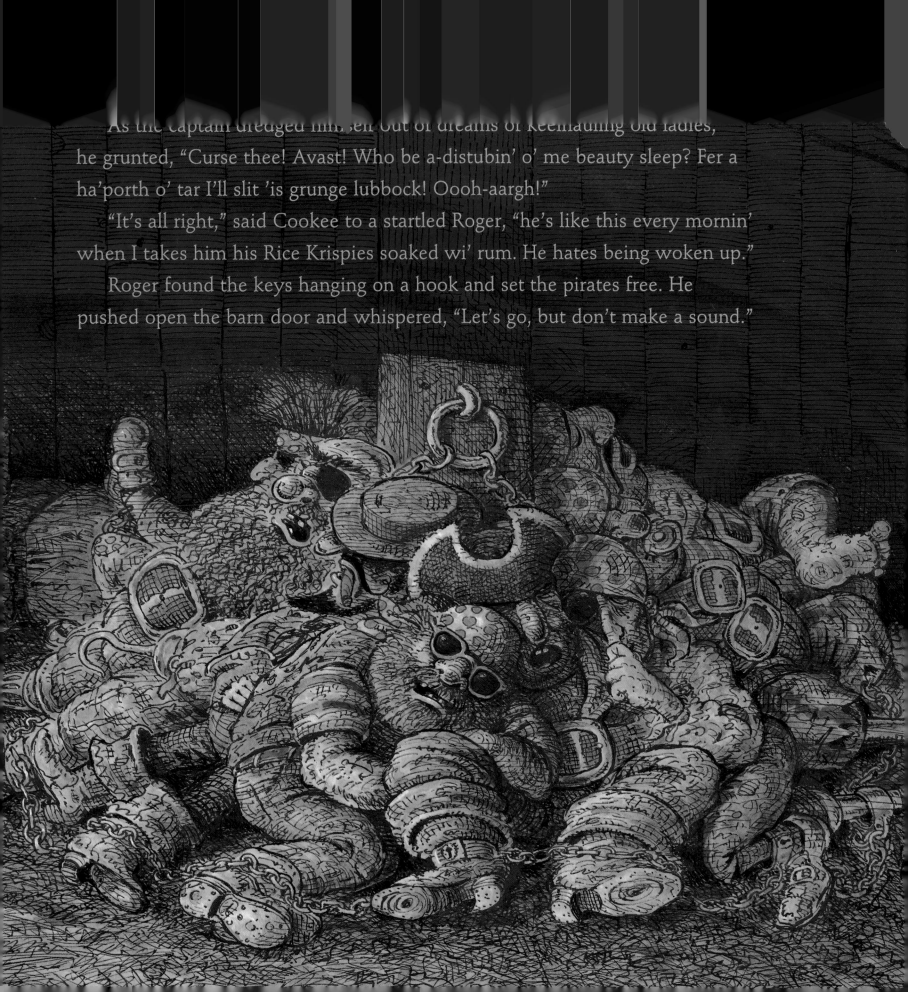

Hooligans!

KABOOM!!!

roared the blunderbuss.

"Get back in the barn you horrible, hairy hooligans!" screamed Roger's mom, who had indeed been watching the barn from behind the curtains.

"Run for it!" said Roger, staying in the shadows. "You won't get a second chance! Over the wall and run for your lives!"

"Back to the ship, me 'earties! The devil is on our 'eels!" bellowed the captain, treading on a rake and blackening his one good eye. "Aargh! I've been hit!" cried the baldy old sea dog. "Be this the end o' Abdul the Skinhead? To die so young! Oooh-aargh! In me prime!"

"Oh, come on!" said Roger. "You'll live. Open your eye and run, peg leg!"

(That did the trick. Abdul was not used to being spoken to in this manner.)

"That's no way to talk to your cap'n, ye wee bilge pump! Men ha' walked the plank for less!"

"Yes, well, we'll discuss it later. Meanwhile, let's get out of here!"

Through the streets
the terrified pirates ran, with
Roger's mom close behind waving
a cutlass. What a sight! What a to-do!
There hadn't been so much excitement since
Sir Walter Raleigh opened the village's first fish
and chip shop! "Help!" "Save us!" "Call a policeman!"
cried the pirates as they ran.

Reaching the quayside, they tumbled and fought to get into
their boat, and began rowing madly for *The Golden Behind*.

"Pull 'ard, ye scunners. Curse ye all! Pull away, or I'll lash 'ee to the
grundell spars an' 'ave 'ee flogged! Oooh-aargh!" threatened the captain
as the rowing boat heaved and lurched wildly across the harbor.

Roger's mom arrived, panting and shouting, and saw Roger in the boat. "Come back here, you lily-livered lot of louts! Grab my Roger, would you? I'll show you!" And looking around for something to throw, she found a wooden bucket, which she hurled high and hard after the escaping pirates. It flew gracefully through the air and landed with a mighty clonk, smack-bang on Cookee's hairy head, knocking him senseless and sending him toppling into the water. What a shot!

"Cookee!" gasped Roger, trying to grab him. But the boat was pulling away. "Man overboard, Captain!" he shouted. "Turn the boat around!"

"No fear!" barked Abdul. "'Tis every man fer 'imself! Pull 'arder, ye dogs! Row, blast 'ee, row! Or there'll be no cocoa in bed tonight! Curse ye! Oooh-aargh!"

"Anyway," said Riff-raff Rafferty, "none of us can swim."

"CAN'T SWIM?" howled Roger. "What sort of pirates are you? Captured by a woman who's knee-high to a grasshopper, then leaving your shipmate to drown! You're a bunch of SOFTIES!" And with these words our hero dived into the shark-infested water and swam toward his friend.
(Well, sardine-infested, actually, but jolly dangerous all the same!)

At the same moment, Roger's mom dived from the quay (she was feeling a bit guilty about clonking the buccaneer on the noodle like that). She and Roger reached Cookee just as he was going down for the third time.

PART V: *Cookee Tells All! Exclusive!*

Roger and his mom managed to pull Cookee back to the quayside.

 With the aid of a boat hook, he was lifted, dripping, out of the water and laid with a squelch on the quay.

 Cookee slowly opened his eyes and began to speak, stopped, removed a sardine from his mouth, then spoke these startling words, "Hello, Ernestine!"

(That was Roger's mom's name.) "It be I, your long-lost husband, and father to your son Roger. That clonk on the nut has given me back my memory and all is now clear. Sweetheart, your beloved Henry (for that was Roger's dad name) is returned!"

Well, bless your little cotton socks, you could have knocked everyone down with a feather! Not Roger's mom though. She was already down. Fainted clean away!

Roger just stood there, gaping like a guppy. "Dad!" was all he could manage.

When his mom recovered her senses she cried, "Hallelujah, it's a miracle! My Henry's come home."

And she did a very strange thing—something Roger had never seen before in all his nine years—she smiled.

Nothing more. She just smiled. Roger was shocked. His mom's face was, well—pretty!

(No Mary Queen of Scots mind you, but not bad!)

Still smiling, she started to cry. Two tears popped out of her eyes, rolled down her cheeks, and plopped onto the dusty quayside.

PART VI: *Yo-ho-ho and Away We Go!*

Meanwhile, well away from all that soppy nonsense, those villainous poltroons, the pirates of Abdul the Skinhead, were off under full sail in the general direction of somewhere a long way away from Roger's mom.

"I'd rather take me chance wi' a two-hundred-gun Spanish Man-o'-War than tackle that woman again! By the fire o' Blackbeard's whiskers!" cursed the captain. "Sail hard, me lads, sail hard! Curse ye! An' next time ye kidnap a cabin boy, take a look-see at his mom first!"

And so, with a final "Oooh-aargh!" they were gone, never to be seen again. (Well, not in this book, anyway!)

PART VII: *The Celebration*

Back on dry land a party was going on. The innkeeper provided the
drink and the storekeeper the food. Both were pleased to be rid
of the pirates, who never paid for anything. There were jugs
of ale for the big 'uns and lemonade for the little 'uns. There was
much singing of sea chanteys and much dancing of sailor-type jigs.
Roger's dad had come home. Roger was happy. Roger's mom
was happy and Roger's dad was happy. (Although it was hard to
tell under all that hair!) Roger's mom told of the tough time

she'd had trying to keep the farm going without him: what a hard
life it had been for Roger and her (You can say that again!
thought Roger) and how unhappy she'd been.
Then the barber sent for his sharpest razor and a bowl of
hot soapy water, and he gave Roger's dad the best shave
he'd had in eight years. (The only one as it happened.)
Without all that grizzle he was quite handsome!
(No Sir Francis Drake mind you, but not bad!)

And so, after a great party, which lasted three days, Roger and his parents said good-bye to everyone and took their leave.

"Come on, Roger and Henry," said Roger's mom. "Let's get you two cleaned up. That farm won't run itself, you know. There's a lot of work to be done!"

Roger and his dad looked at each other and burst out laughing. "Aye-aye, Cap'n!" they shouted. "Aye-aye!"

And the three of them went home.

THE END

For the Conways of Elvan Lodge

Second U.S. edition 1995

Library of Congress Cataloging-in-Publication Data

McNaughton, Colin.
Jolly Roger and the pirates of Captain Abdul / Colin McNaughton.—
2nd U.S. ed.
Summary: Eager to leave the hardships of home, Roger becomes
part of a pirate crew, only to discover his long-lost father.
ISBN 1-56402-512-8
[1. Pirates—Fiction.   2. Humorous stories.]   I. Title.
PZ7.M23256Jo   1995
[Fic]—dc20   94-25703

2 4 6 8 10 9 7 5 3 1

Printed in Hong Kong

The pictures in this book were done in watercolor and ink.

Candlewick Press
2067 Massachusetts Avenue
Cambridge, Massachusetts 02140

COLIN MCNAUGHTON has been drawing monsters and dinosaurs, giants and pirates since he was a boy. His sense of humor remains as childlike as ever, which perhaps explains why he is so popular with young readers. He has published more than fifty titles in the United States and England, including *Making Friends with Frankenstein* and *Captain Abdul's Pirate School.*